PARALLEL UNIVERSE

AN INTERACTIVE TIME ADVENTURE

Written by
NICOLA BAXTER

Illustrated by
MIKE TAYLOR

SCHOLASTIC CANADA LTD.

© 1996 Franklin Watts
First published in Canada by
Scholastic Canada Ltd.
123 Newkirk Road
Richmond Hill
Ontario L4C 3G5

Editors: Kyla Barber & Rosemary McCormick
Designer: Eljay Crompton

Canadian Cataloguing in Publication Data
Baxter, Nicola
Parallel universe : an interactive adventure
ISBN 0-590-12382-3
1. Picture puzzles — Juvenile literature. 2. Civilization — Juvenile literature.
I. Taylor, Mike, 1949-
II. Title.

GV1507.P47B39 1997   j793.73   C97–930379–6

CONTENTS

...TRANSMISSION FROM THE CONTROLLER, INTERGALACTIC CENTER FOR PLANETARY CO-ORDINATION (I.C.P.C.)...

Traveler, your mission is urgent and dangerous. To accept it puts you in great peril. Yet the fate of the universe as we know it is in your hands.

From your studies of galactic geography you will know that our planet has an identical twin—a world exactly like our own, which exists in a parallel universe. Everything that has happened on Earth, throughout history, has happened on that parallel planet. Recently we have discovered that this synchronicity is vital. These paired planets must remain exactly matched if our universe is to survive.

You will have heard of the major cosmic accident near Zeta XII. Minutes ago we learned that the first shock waves from the disaster area caused minor damage to our twin planet. It seems that a number of unrelated objects in the parallel world have slipped uncontrollably through time and space. Fortunately, the position has stabilized. The objects have come to rest, but are now out of place historically.

Our technicians calculate that only hours remain before the situation deteriorates. From the moment the parallel planet begins to fail, our own world is doomed. It is vital that all of the objects are returned to their original eras. All our futures depend on it.

Your mission will take you into thirteen time zones. To avoid further damage to the delicate balance of the planet, in each zone you have been provided with a *cyberform, a shell-body cloned from one of the inhabitants of that time and place. You will need to find this cyberform first. It will exactly mirror a being from each zone except that it will be holding a shiny object. That object masks the latest development in reflective technology: a device with which the **time-slipped objects may be mirrored back to their correct time and place.

As you enter the zone, my written instructions will give you useful data to aid you in your search. You have exactly one hour in each zone to find twenty misplaced objects. If you fail, you cannot move on to the next era. Your mission will end. Finally, you must find a time portal through which to leave the zone. Portals on the parallel planet have a blue, sparkling appearance that you will come to recognize easily.

> **To summarize, your tasks are threefold:**
> - **Locate your waiting cyberform, which holds a reflective object;**
> - **Identify the twenty time-slipped objects;**
> - **Find the sparkling blue time portal that leads to the next zone.**

Traveler, beware of flying objects as you enter the parallel universe and turn the page to begin your mission. The hopes of a whole universe go with you. Good luck.

TRANSMISSION SUSPENDED . . .

---

* cyberform: a twin that appears as a mirror image

** time-slipped object: an object that does not belong in this historical period

THE GREATEST CIVILIZATION UNDER THE SUN

Traveler, you are in Thebes, Egypt, in northern Africa. It is 1400 BC. In this heat and dust, in a city teeming with people, it is a matter of urgency to find your cyberform. It is male, cloned from a guard in conversation on a shady rooftop. His mirror image awaits you on a bustling public street.

The river before you is the Nile. Its importance to these people and to your mission cannot be overstated. As prosperous citizens brush past you with their purchases of finery, you may not realize that you are standing in the middle of a desert land where rain may fall on only one day in the year. This great civilization depends entirely for its survival and success on the nearby waters of the Nile.

Do not be careless with water during your stay—you will draw attention to yourself at once. Every drop that is used here has to be raised from the river, using a simple crane, or channeled through a basic irrigation system. There is no plumbing as we understand it.

The sun here is relentless. Be careful. Only the wealthy, with their shady courtyard pools, can afford to employ slaves to fan them constantly as they are entertained by musicians and dancers. This civilization has only basic technology—no electricity or steam power. Huge numbers of slaves supply the energy in this city. The Egyptians' ambitious building projects and the lavish lifestyles of the rich could not continue without them.

The fastest way to search is on foot. The wooden-wheeled carts of this region make slow progress. In fact, the Nile also provides an important means of transport. Boats of wood and reeds carry not only people and goods but also the huge blocks of stone needed to build the great temples on the riverbanks.

The symbols carved and painted on walls and pillars are not decoration but writing. Each tiny picture of a bird or object stands for a different sound. Do not waste time translating this, but, as always, be alert for anything that looks out of place and time.

To find all the time-slipped objects, you will need to enter the private homes and gardens of important people. Do not pause to ask or explain. Walk purposefully, as if on an errand for a senior official, and you are unlikely to be challenged. But you will need to notice even the tiniest details as you swiftly pass.

Remember, you have twenty time-slipped objects to find within one hour. I must advise you not to eat or drink during your stay, in view of the heat and lack of refrigeration. One last point—beware of the sleek cats and dogs kept as pets by the privileged few. They may sense your true nature.

Your time has begun . . .

THE HEART OF AN EMPIRE

Traveler, your unfamiliar appearance will be instantly obvious here! Find your cyberform viewing the scene from across the pool in these splendid baths. It is AD 100. You are in Rome, Italy, the capital of a vast empire. These men are confident and ruthless. You cannot afford to make mistakes.

The ease and luxury that you see before you is not surprising. These people enjoy enormous power. The Romans control all of southern Europe, as far north as Britain. They rule northern Africa, including Egypt. In large areas of Asia, too, their authority is supreme. And Rome is at the center of it all. From here, the Emperor Trajan controls an empire soon to reach its greatest extent.

Yet this power, as so often happens, is at the expense of others. Slaves from all over the empire are bought and sold to serve the ruling classes. Very few women have control over their own lives. And millions of people throughout the empire obey the dictates of an alien power that calls them barbarians.

Yet as you look around you, you will see clues to some of the advantages that the Romans have brought to far-flung lands. Educated Romans have introduced reading and writing where no written language existed before. Many buildings, like this one, have piped water and underground central heating. Impressive feats of engineering—roads criss-crossing the empire, water carried on aqueducts across dry lands—have brought undreamed of luxury to a few trusted inhabitants of conquered regions.

In this soothing atmosphere, you may be tempted to relax. Baths like these are to be found in most towns. Here Roman men can exercise and rest as well as meet socially to talk business. Sports and weight-training keep them fit, while slaves bathe them and bring them refreshments.

But be on your guard at all times! This society holds its power through force. Roman rulers must be vigilant. Uprisings and assassinations are not unknown. If you are caught as a spy, your punishment will be swift and merciless. Worse, hundreds of people may enjoy watching you die at the hands of a gladiator or torn apart by wild animals.

Remember, although you will find much that is familiar here, this society is very unlike our own. True, there are skilled artists and engineers, but there is no electrical power. No factories for mass production. Only natural fabrics and materials are known. These men may feel all-powerful, but their understanding of the universe as we know it is poor indeed.

Your training reminds you that this empire will not stand for ever. Less than 400 years from now, barbarians will enter the gates of Rome. Yet Rome has left us legacies that time may never erase. The language of the Romans, Latin, has left many traces in our own tongue. *Tempus fugit*, traveler—time flies. May you be as swift.

9

THE POWER AND THE FURY

Traveler, scan this document rapidly and proceed with extreme caution. You have arrived in the year AD 793. You are on the windswept northeast coast of Britain. The screaming of dying men, the shrieking of gulls and the clash of weapons fills the air, while thick smoke, whipped by the salt wind, stings your eyes. Find your cyberform *at once*—then run for your life. Your cyberform is cloned from a young monk who, even now, is running desperately, seconds from death by the sword of a Norseman. Your mirror-image cyberform is fleeing too, clasping a silver plate.

To find the twenty time-slipped objects and move safely to the next zone, you *must* evade capture. I recommend that you escape into the sea, then swim stealthily around the ships when they have all landed.

This may seem a small and isolated settlement, but news of this Viking attack will send shock waves throughout Europe. The remote monastery of Lindisfarne is famous as a place of Christian learning. "From the fury of the Norsemen, good Lord deliver us!" has long been a prayer in the coastal villages of Britain, but never before has an important religious community been attacked. The threat of Viking invasion menaces much of the continent—and that threat has just become more real.

It may be June, but you will find these northern waters icy and rough. The Vikings are fearless sailors. They voyage thousands of miles in boats built with only simple iron tools. They have no instruments to help them navigate or safety aids if disaster

strikes. In the boats themselves, your search should be easy, for their contents are meager. The rowers sit on chests containing their few possessions. Food and barrels of fresh water fill the center of the crowded boat. There is just room for weapons and shields, but no protection for the men from the lashing waves and wind.

Without charts, lights, or radar, the Vikings rely on their extraordinary seamanship to cross great expanses of water. They are brave fighters, too. Brandishing heavy swords, spears, and bows, they are protected only by their helmets, round shields, and clothing of wool and leather.

These Norsemen come from Denmark. The fertile farmlands of Britain promise food and rich pickings to take back to a country that cannot support its people. But the rough woolen robe your cyberform wears shows that life for the monks of Lindisfarne is also harsh. In this remote place, they grow their own food, gather fuel for the fires that supply their only heat, and laboriosly copy and decorate Christian texts by hand.

You know, as the doomed monks cannot, that in the centuries to come the Norsemen too will become Christians and their leaders will rule wisely over much of Europe—but on this day of terror, expect no mercy.

11

A SERMON IN STONE

Traveler, you are in Chartres, France, in the dust and muddle of a medieval building site. It is 1218. Keep your wits about you. Modern safety regulations do not apply on this site! You will need to find your cyberform quickly, as exploring the building and its surroundings will take time. Your cyberform is cloned from a workman risking life and limb, high above the solid ground. His mirror-image, holding a reflective object, is only slightly lower.

You should find it easy to mingle on foot with the people who come to marvel at the cathedral, but I must warn you not to draw attention to yourself by unusual behavior. Among these people, everyone knows his or her place in society. Behavior considered odd or different may be seen as the work of the devil. Take care that you do not join those misfits burned at the stake as witches for some harmless eccentricity.

In many ways these people have a very uncertain existence. Knowledge of medicine is limited and life can be painful and short. There is little time to relax. Very few people can read or write. Wealthy landowners and the bishops and clergy have great power over ordinary people. Everyone needs to believe that the seeming chaos of the world is part of a greater order. Christian faith promises that everything is part of God's plan. The ordered beauty of the cathedral gives a kind of picture of the harmony of all things in God's creation.

When you stand before the great west front of the cathedral, looking up at the decorated stonework towering above you (and keeping an eye out for carelessly dropped tools or stone!), you may wonder how such a magnificent building can be built without electrical tools and machines, or even steel for scaffolding. The massive lumps of stone have to be brought miles on river barges or in ox-drawn carts.

The builders plan, design, and build without a full under-standing of engineering to work out the stresses and strains on the massive pillars and arching vaults. What they do have, and have in great supply, is faith.

Avoid the bishop and senior clergy. They have sharp eyes and wits. Many great churches and cities thrive on the money of pilgrims—devout Christians who travel on horseback or on foot to pray before a relic, a fragment of bone or cloth from the body of a saint, in the hope of God's blessing.

The building work before you comes after a disastrous fire in 1194. For a few days the future of the cathedral and the city was uncertain. Then the cathedral's most famous relic, said to be part of the gown of the Virgin Mary, was found, miraculously unburned, and everyone breathed a sigh of relief. The city could expect its floods of visitors once more. A new future would rise from the ashes of the past.

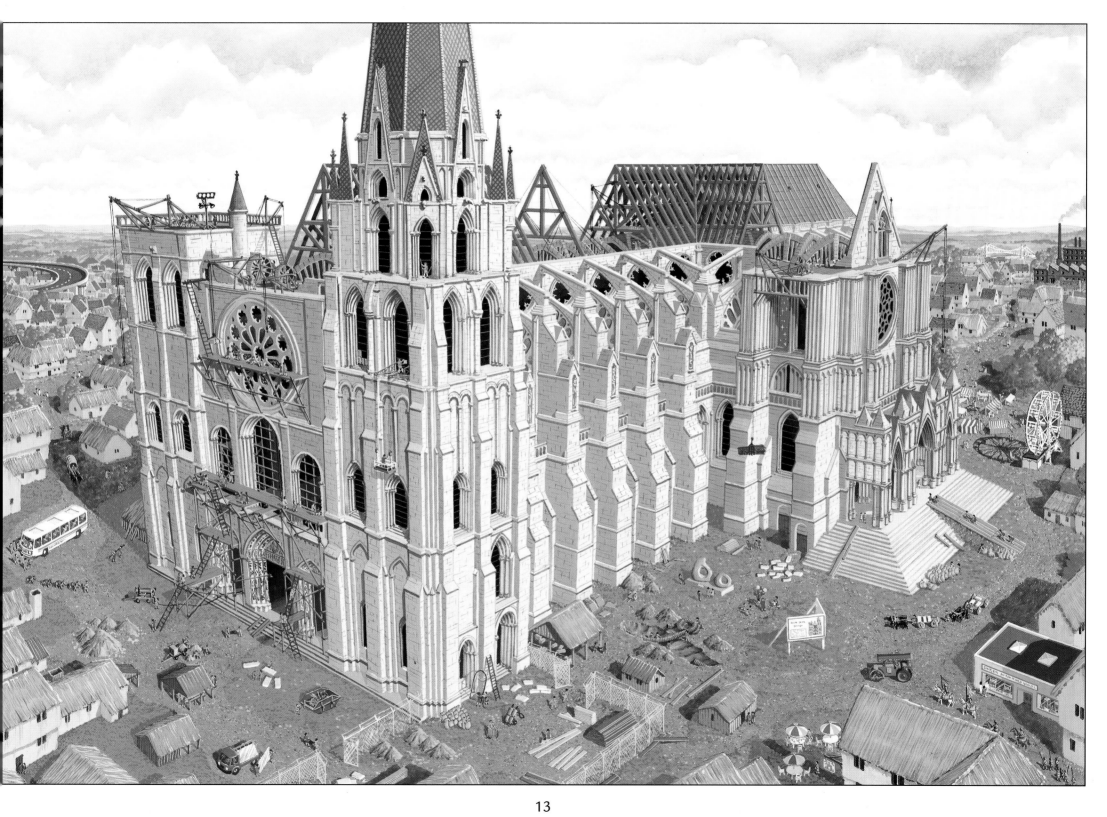

13

DISCOVERY AND REDISCOVERY

Traveler, this time there is no crowded street in which to hide yourself. This is a private home in Florence, Italy. The year is 1492. Luckily your cyberform is easy to find. Cloned from a young man talking on a balcony, he carries a shiny plate. As a servant, you will be able to pass through this room without notice. But keep your wits about you. It is vital that you do not draw attention to yourself by showing undue curiosity.

You are in the home of a wealthy and powerful family at a time when enormous and exciting changes are taking place. For hundreds of years the Church has been the center of scholarship. Now rich patrons are paying for research into science, art, music, and astronomy. There is a great curiosity about the world, which is as strange and unknown at this time as the furthest reaches of the galaxy were in the twentieth century.

In this one year, Columbus has crossed the Atlantic and reached the West Indies. Although still with limited knowledge, map-makers have created a globe to represent the Earth. Young Michelangelo is creating wonderful works of art, right here in Florence. Leonardo da Vinci has designed a flying machine. True, it will be hundreds of years before any machine will successfully take to the air, but we cannot help but admire his vision and imagination.

In this year, Lorenzo the Magnificent, of the Medici, the most important family in Florence, has died. The genius of rich and powerful men like Lorenzo is to use what is best from the past while investing in the future. This time zone has been called the *Renaissance*, meaning rebirth, because there is a great surge of interest in the style and success of the Roman and Greek empires. But classical learning is simply a starting point. These people are as interested in the future as we are.

The enthusiasm for the new ideas of the Italian Renaissance will spread like wildfire throughout Europe, but perhaps here in Florence it has its finest flowering. Throughout the city beautiful buildings are being constructed, statues decorate the public squares, and business is brisk among the merchants.

The wealth of the Medici family has come from their business interests—all the more impressive at a time when there are no computers or telephones to keep track of a business empire. Clerks toil with quill and ink among their record books and rolls of parchment.

Remember to lower your eyes and show respect as you move about the room. This wealthy family relies on an army of servants for its comfort. In the days before electricity, it is they who do all the labor required to heat and light the house, prepare the food and drink, and entertain their employers.

The explosion of learning has not improved everyone's life, but there is a feeling of excitement and change in the air. For those with a skill to sell, who can find a wealthy patron, a more pleasant life beckons. Find the twenty time-slipped items as quickly as you can, for this world is changing as quickly as your own.

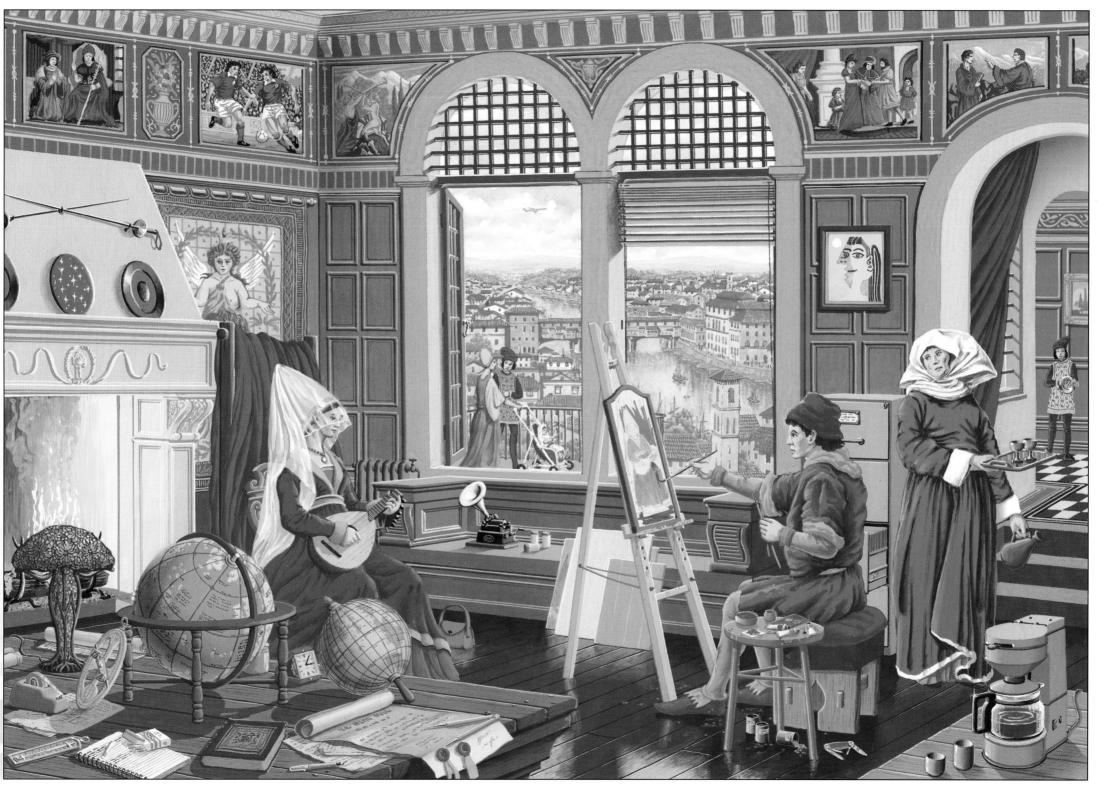

15

WORLDS COLLIDE

Traveler, you have arrived at the fateful meeting of two worlds. You are standing in Tenochtitlán, Mexico, the capital of the great Aztec empire. It is 1519 – less than thirty years since the first European set foot on the American continent. Under the burning Mexican sun, the crowd chatters excitedly, but you perhaps sense the unease and suspicion in the air.

Find your cyberform. It will give you an excellent view. Cloned from a child seated on his father's shoulders, the mirror-image cyberform has the same vantage point, but carries a reflective object.

Amidst the glitter of the occasion, your eyes will be drawn to the powerful faces of two men. Riding at the head of six hundred soldiers, the black-bearded Cortés, a Spanish fortune-hunter, has risked crossing the Atlantic by sailing ship to follow rumors of riches on the uncharted mainland of the Americas. He expected a battle, not a welcome fit for a god.

Do not gaze too boldly on the face of the man before him, for he is thought to be a god-king. Montezuma, the Aztec emperor, surrounded by his golden court, seems all-powerful. Yet he is making a tragic mistake. Among the Aztec gods, Quetzalcoatl, god of the wind, has a white face, a black beard, and a plumed headdress. Legend tells that this figure from the past will return, bringing good fortune. But it is not the past that stands before Montezuma. It is the future, and the future is terrible.

You may not find it easy to locate time-slipped objects in the Aztec capital, for it seems a city of the future, built in the middle of a lake, with a regular grid of streets like a modern metropolis. The inhabitants appear to enjoy a civilized life. Aqueducts carry fresh water into the center, while gold jewelry and ornaments are not hard to find.

The best way for you to explore is by boat, following the series of canals, in a simple Aztec canoe. As you penetrate farther into the city, you may notice features more typical of an earlier civilization. The Aztecs have not yet discovered the wheel or the use of iron. They have no written language—their documents show information in the form of pictures.

And take care to hide your reactions to religious practices, hard as that may be. Remember, as Cortés did not, that you are a visitor from another world, here neither to judge nor to influence. The Aztecs believe that daily sacrifices of human lives ensure that the sun god rises each morning. The stone steps of the temples run red with human blood.

Relish this rare glimpse of a doomed city. The Spanish *conquistadores* do not have your knowledge. Within a few years, the Aztecs will almost have been wiped out by fighting and European disease. Yet in our own time, high above Mexico City, built on the site of Tenochtitlán, flies the red, white, and green flag of modern Mexico, showing the image of an eagle perched on a cactus. A little piece of the Aztec legend lives on.

A DOOR CLOSES

Traveler, find your cyberform quickly, for visitors have begun to outstay their welcome in seventeenth-century Japan. It is 1633. You find yourself in the bustling harbor of Nagasaki. Your cyberform is cloned from a servant, bowing respectfully. It carries refreshments in shiny containers.

Moving through the port, you will feel the tension in the air. It is less than a hundred years since the first Europeans visited Japan, although the news of its riches had reached the ears of adventurers some years before. It was Japan that Christopher Columbus was seeking when he made his historic journey. Indeed, to his dying day, he believed that he had found it.

For Europeans the journey by sea to this very different land is still long and dangerous. But it brings great rewards. European goods can be traded for silk, spices, porcelain, and silver. And imagine for a moment the wonder with which these two peoples view each other. To the Japanese, Europeans are hairy creatures with red faces. In turn, visitors find little that they can understand: a strange language, a different way of writing, and unfamiliar customs.

As you know well, traveler, meetings between two worlds are often difficult, especially when one side sets out to change the way of life of the other. Christian missionaries have had great success in converting the Japanese from their own beliefs. Now they are in danger. This exchange of goods and ideas is about to end.

The military ruler of Japan, the shogun, fears that outside influences challenge his power. Very soon now only the Dutch, based on a tiny island in Nagasaki harbor, will be able to trade with the Japanese. Christianity will be completely outlawed. For most purposes, Japan will be cut off from the rest of the world for the next two hundred years.

The Japanese themselves will not be allowed to travel abroad. If they leave the country, they may not return. Although they are skilled sailors, sea-going ships will not be built. Only smaller boats, able to travel around the coast, will be permitted.

But do not believe that the Japan you see around you will remain frozen in time. Undisturbed by the rest of the world, Japan can look forward to two centuries of peace in which the country will change and grow. Just as in Europe, power here will gradually move from military commanders, the legendary *samurai*, to the merchants and money-makers.

Be cautious, but enjoy exploring this lively and thriving society. Wealthy Japanese live in beautiful homes, where they can enjoy painting, poetry, and music. Exquisite porcelain, lacquer work, and silk brocades are finer than those found in Europe. By keeping its visitors at arm's length, Japan controls its own fate. Our fate is in *your* hands. You know your task . . . you have more than time to lose.

OFF WITH HIS HEAD!

Traveler, on a cold January morning in 1793, you find yourself in Paris, France. A royal execution is about to take place.

Although there are hundreds of soldiers to keep order, emotions are running high. Find your cyberform quickly. He has been cloned from a cavalry officer, facing the guillotine. The cyberform is similarly positioned, holding aloft a reflective object. On horseback, you will have a fine view of all that happens. The rank of officer will allow you to move freely among the crowd, seeking the time-slipped objects.

In the misty morning light, the condemned man's face is white as he stands below the guillotine. He opens his mouth to speak. At once every drummer in the square begins to play, drowning out the King's last words. The noise is deafening. Even if they could hear the speech, these people are unlikely to attempt a rescue. Things have come too far for that.

For nearly four years, a revolution has been taking place in France. The country has been ruled by the King and wealthy noblemen, who lived in luxury while most people endured great poverty. When the King tried to increase taxes to pay for foreign wars, the people revolted. The storming of the Bastille prison in 1789 was one of the first acts of unrest in the French Revolution.

All around you, the imposing buildings of Paris are boarded up and those noblemen who have escaped the anger of the people hide behind closed doors. It is not wealth itself that the revolutionaries hate, but the fact that the comfortable lives of a few are built on the misery of many. The flags flying around the square will look familiar. Revolutionaries show support for their cause by wearing red caps with a blue and white rosette. Their red, white, and blue flag is still the flag of France in our time.

Amid the thundering of the drums, the famous guillotine waits for its royal victim. The world waits too. There is no radio and television, but newspapers have become an important way of spreading news quickly. This news will add to the feeling that is growing throughout the western world that ordinary people, not just the rich and powerful, have a right to make decisions about their government and lives. The revolutionaries around you shout out their belief in "Liberty, Equality, Fraternity."

In seconds, news of the King's death will surge out of Paris to the farthest corners of Europe and the wider world, as fast, at least, as a horse and rider can take it.

Great scientific discoveries are being made daily, but a use has yet to be found for the strange sparks called electricity. And the recently invented steam engine has still to revolutionize industry and transport.

Make the most of this moment when a precarious order reigns. Your task may be more difficult when the shining blade has fallen, and the country no longer has a king.

21

THE MIGHTY MACHINE

Traveler, you have jumped fifty years to a country undergoing a different kind of revolution. Great advances in industry and farming will change the way the world works forever. You are in Manchester, England, in 1845.

Your cyberform is cloned from a farm worker digging in a field. His mirror image prepares to take more sweeping action around his cottage. Find your cyberform quickly, for there is much to see and learn.

As you look up from your work, you may feel the eyes of the landowner upon you, but you need not fear discovery. He has little interest in one man and the small amount of rent he pays for his cottage. He has bigger plans. This morning, he gazes across his land and imagines his new factory, where steam-powered machines will weave more cotton cloth in one week than a whole village of craftsmen and women could produce in a year.

The mill will have a prime position. The finished cloth will no longer need to reach its market by slow, horse-drawn carts and packhorses traveling along rutted roads. Instead it will be loaded straight onto a barge on the nearby canal and follow the network of waterways that now crosses the country. Soon the new railway, too, will reach to every city and port.

In the fields, farmworkers do not realize that their way of life is threatened. Already, there have been changes in the country-side. Although machinery has not yet eased the back-breaking work, crops are now rotated to keep the land fertile. Common land has been fenced in. But whatever else changes, the farming year will always have its own rhythm. Laborers work from dawn to dusk, whatever the weather, and season follows season as it always has.

Enter the growing industrial city with care. It is not a healthy place to linger. A cloud of black smoke hangs over the mills, where the clatter of machinery never stops. Day after day, week after week, workers labor to serve the mighty machines.

You are advised not to enter the factories. Most mill owners show less concern for their workers' safety than for their own profits. Even small children work long hours at dangerous jobs. Avoid the streets when the whistle blows for the end of a shift. Then the narrow alleys are choked with hundreds of workers of all ages, wearily walking home to their cramped, brick houses.

As you explore, it will become clear why this country is leading the world into the industrial age. In this small area, coal mines supply the fuel for the steam engines and iron ore is dug to make the huge machinery. Speed and profit are the order of the day.

Not everyone welcomes the regular work and wages that the factories bring. You may meet some of those who protest against the coming of the machines. But do not allow yourself to be drawn into an argument. They cannot know, as you do, that their way of life has changed forever.

WAY OUT WEST

Traveler, incredible as this may seem, the bustling town in which you find yourself did not exist ten years ago. Then, mile upon mile of unspoiled country stretched as far as the eye could see. You are in Oregon, in the far west of the United States. The year is 1876.

The people here are wary of strangers. It has been known for them to act first and ask questions later. Find your cyberform at once. It has been cloned from a woman watching the unloading of a stagecoach. Her mirror-image is in fact looking at a mirror-image!

Around you a country is growing at an extraordinary speed. Oregon itself only became a state in 1859 and the map of the United States is still very different from the one we know today. As you go along the wooden sidewalk, snippets of conversations in many languages meet your ears. Fortunately, your training equips you to understand them all. Settlers have come from China, Africa, Russia, and most of Europe. Many were drawn here by the very things that first caused Europeans to set foot on American soil: the lure of gold and the promise of a better life.

That promise is something that the original people of this country find it hard to believe in. Many Native Americans first welcomed the newcomers, only to find their whole way of life threatened by different ideas and customs. Misunderstandings and broken promises have caused many conflicts. The future seems bleak for the oldest Americans of all.

Do not be alarmed if everyone you meet seems to be carrying a firearm. In spite of the best efforts of the sheriff, these are rough and ready times. Greed and whiskey are powerful forces. Every man wishes to be able to defend his property, especially if it includes gold. Since gold was discovered in California in 1849, thousands of prospectors have made the journey west. Today, you are probably more likely to be kicked by a prospector's mule than gunned down in cold blood!

Stay on the sidewalk if you wish to avoid the worst of the mud, especially when a horse and rider gallop past. They may look like the legendary Pony Express, but the coming of the telegraph has put an end to those dramatic rides. Now news can travel from the east coast to the west in a matter of seconds, although letters must travel more slowly, by train.

The railroad, finished only seven years ago, is now the best way of crossing the continent. The stained and battered covered wagons that made the months-long journey from the east are almost a thing of the past.

You may find this zone more familiar than those you have visited before. You are still in an age before electricity or the motor car but you have reached the age of photography. You may well have seen scenes very like this one in your own time. However, photographs cannot entirely prepare you for the sounds and (as there is no proper drainage) the smells of another time and place . . .

GOODBYE TO ALL THAT

Traveler, it is August 1st, 1914. Your search in this zone will take you on board the famous steamship *Mauretania* as she prepares to sail for New York from her dock in Liverpool, England. Work rapidly—it will spell disaster for your mission if you fail to disembark in time!

Your cyberform has been cloned from a member of the ship's crew. He is on board, ensuring that the first class passengers have a clear view during the crossing. The mirror-image that you are looking for is on the dockside, conducting a treat for the passengers' ears rather than their eyes. Find him quickly. The last passengers and goods are now being loaded and the luxury liner will soon be underway.

Once again, you are in possession of privileged information. Under no circumstances must you share the following with anyone you meet. Few of the ship's two thousand passengers, or those who have come to wave them off, can know how soon the world around them will change.

As the fastest trans-Atlantic liner in the world, the *Mauretania* can reach New York in 4 days, 17 hours, and 21 minutes. In the days before passenger aircraft, there is no quicker way to travel between Europe and America. But this steamship cannot outrun world events. Three days from now, Britain will declare war on Germany and the First World War will begin. Europe will be split apart by a conflict more terrible than these people can imagine. A united Europe will seem unthinkable for many years to come.

You are looking at a society that is strictly organized. On the *Mauretania* there are first, second, and third class passengers. Eating in separate dining rooms, strolling on separate decks, they will never meet. Your uniform will allow you to pass among all classes without question. The way of life you see will not survive the events of the next four years.

You need to understand that many people suffer restrictions because of their class or sex. Revealing your surprise at what you see will not further your mission. In both Britain and the United States, women are still campaigning to be allowed to vote. It is unheard of for a woman to work in a senior job and most do not work outside the home. Decorum is strictly observed. Women's long skirts, huge hats, and parasols protect them from the sun and the gaze of men's eyes!

But notice that already the world seems a smaller place. The *Mauretania* has the newly developed ship-to-shore radio, while on land telephones are becoming popular. The Panama Canal was finished this year, cutting 7,000 miles (11,200 km) off the journey from the Atlantic to the Pacific. Early motor cars are beginning to replace horses. In America, Henry Ford is producing the Model T car, putting car travel within the reach of ordinary families.

The *Mauretania* and many of her passengers will survive the war, but she represents an age that is passing. Find the time-slipped objects within the hour, or our own age is under an even greater threat.

LIGHTS, MUSIC, ACTION!

Traveler, you are in a place where dreams are made. It is Hollywood, California. The time is 1936. In this setting, your appearance is not likely to cause surprise, but you will need to find your cyberform and its reflective object in order to mirror the time-slipped items back to their own zones. Your cyberform has been cloned from an artist painting a background. His mirror image holds a container in which a fantasy is played out.

You will need your wits about you to sift reality from illusion in Hollywood. Illusion, after all, is what this place is all about. It originally attracted film-makers because of the long hours of daylight and the variety of scenery within easy reach. Nearby there is desert for tales of ancient Egypt, mountains for dramatic stories of exploration, the coast for seafaring sagas, and, of course, wide open spaces for the ever-popular Westerns. Even space adventures, still only a dream even for scientists, are filmed nearby. So, in their own way, movie-goers are time travelers too, but the worlds they visit exist only in California!

In its short history, movie-making has opened up a world of entertainment that everyone can enjoy. Many working people find that they have more time for leisure now. At the movies, exciting stories of struggle and success make all things seem possible. Films give information, too, showing pictures of people and places that the viewers could never see for themselves, and news programs make international reports seem as real as life in the street outside.

These days it is not only the rich and powerful who are able to influence people's lives. Movie stars, not pop singers or politicians, are the popular heroes and heroines of the day. Magazines give the latest gossip to adoring fans, who hurry to copy their idols' clothes and hairstyles.

Of course, some features of the stars' lives are not within reach of their followers. Air travel is too expensive for most people, and automobiles are still a sign of financial success. But electrical appliances are beginning to make running a home easier for everyone. Families can live in a style that in past times would have been possible only with dozens of servants. Even so, thousands of young people dream of living the luxurious lifestyles of the filmstars.

I'm sure that I do not need to warn you to be careful as you move about the studio, especially near the cameras. We cannot risk your mission, now so nearly completed, being recorded. And be careful with the early film equipment. Cameras and lights are heavy and easily damaged. The microchip, which will allow machines to be small and portable, has not yet been invented. Film-makers have to manage without the aid of computers and electronic wizardry.

Look carefully at everything. This is not a world in which you can believe what you see. After eleven time zones, your instinct for what is out of place should be at its sharpest. In this factory of fantasy, that is just as well.

THE FINAL CHALLENGE

Traveler, congratulations! You have located the 240 time-slipped objects and sent them spinning back to their proper place in time and space. At this moment you should be enjoying the thanks of a grateful universe. I'm afraid that is not possible—yet.

The shock waves from the cosmic accident on Zeta XII had their worst effect on eras nearer our own. You are now back in the present, in an airport in southern Africa. Unfortunately, twenty objects that were reflected back to this zone have failed to reach their destination. Some have been lost entirely. Others have arrived back without some vital component. These incomplete objects are as dangerous to our existence as the items that are totally absent. As you know, the tiniest difference in the structure of a time zone can result in catastrophic changes in the future.

So damaging has been the reflection failure in this zone that the twentieth century is frozen. Time stands still. Nothing in the universe can go forward until this final task is completed. And for that we need you, traveler. Only you have the experience and skills to help us in this last challenge.

Your mission to date has been demanding, I know. But we are faced with no other option. Only you have the necessary knowledge of the 240 time-slipped objects to identify those items that have not returned. Only you can describe them in sufficient detail for us to locate them in whatever pocket of far-flung space debris they lie.

This time your task is even more challenging. You are not seeking objects that are out of place, but objects that are *not there at all!* You have no need of a cyberform in this zone. People stand fixed in the positions they held when the shock wave hit. You can pass freely among them without being seen or heard. And this time, *we* will replace the objects—as soon as we have your descriptions.

Examine every clue. Think carefully about the objects you have already found and consider which ones might find their home in this time and place. Look out for anything that is out of the ordinary, unexplained, or incomplete. During your mission, your senses will have become alert to every detail. Make the most of your powers now. Above all, work as quickly as you can. To our knowledge, this phenomenon has not occurred before. We cannot say how long this equilibrium can be sustained before permanent damage is caused.

One final warning: when you have found the twentieth object, leave the zone by the time portal at all possible speed. Your presence may upset the delicate universal mechanism that will allow the sands of time to run once more . . .

A PUZZLE FROM TIMES PAST

Traveler, you have done well. An official ceremony of welcome and thanks will greet you on your return to I.C.P.C. The entire galaxy is in your debt. An escort is on its way to bring you back to the Center in fitting style. No doubt your final report is completed and you have time to relax. Perhaps as you await your escort, you may be amused by this little puzzle.

You may remember that until the late twentieth century, when time travel became possible, historians attempted to capture a sense of the past in repositories called *museums*. By collecting together objects from earlier times, they attempted to teach their own generations about the lives of those who went before.

You may smile at this quaint idea. Of course, their understanding could never be complete by our standards. Viewing a piece of ancient Egyptian jewelry through a dusty glass cannot give a true sense of the times in which it was made and worn. They could only glimpse the past in their imaginations, fired by the beauty of isolated objects. But we should not look down on them. They did their best with the methods available. And we learned our respect for the past from them.

The museum storeroom in which you find yourself was recently discovered by inter-galactic archaeologists working in Germany.

It appears to be the collection of an eccentric millionaire that was to be displayed for her eyes alone. This collector was not interested in one particular era or subject. She chose objects that intrigued and delighted her. Some are priceless works of art. Others are everyday items from an enormous range of eras.

It may not take you long to realize that you have already encountered the objects in these displays. On your travels through time and space, you may have glimpsed them as you searched, or examined them in more detail as you completed your mission. As you move among the objects, they may strike a chord in your memory, bringing back images from the extra-ordinary journey you have undertaken.

Except for one object. Yes, strangely enough, one object alone is unknown to you. You did not meet it on your travels. I wonder, can you identify it?

Take your time, traveler. Your mission is over and we can ask no more of you. But perhaps you will enjoy lingering among these long-forgotten collections, enjoying these old friends— and discovering the one intriguing stranger.

33

MISSION DEBRIEFING

TIME ZONE 1: THEBES, EGYPT 1400 BC

- Your cyberform is a soldier, standing with a shiny shield in the street by a wall.
- The Egyptian sun is very bright, but sunglasses will not be available for hundreds of years.
- The Egyptians have discovered that they can tell the time—with sundials; wrist-watches will not be worn until 1887. ● Water is precious in this climate but it is not available from a tap.
- Egyptian entertaining is lavish, but this hostess cart is strictly a 20th-century aid. ● It will be nearly 3,000 years before a medieval suit of armor is worn. ● Military discipline is important to the Egyptians, but this soldier is from World War II. ● Hunting is popular in ancient Egypt, but hunters do not wear modern safari suits! ● Pictures of musicians appear among Egyptian hieroglyphs, but the amplifier is from the 1970s. ● Dancing is also popular, but a ballerina in a tutu will not be seen until much later. ● Thousands of years before the gasoline-driven engine, a boat with an outboard motor is just a dream. ● Compared with the ancient Egyptian ladder next to it, the stepladder is clearly a much more modern version.
- Gas or electric lamps are completely unknown here. Flaming torches light the Egyptians' way. ● This dynasty uses hieroglyphs. Hindu-Arabic numerals will not be in use for nearly 2,000 years. ● The hieroglyph of an ice-cream cone is attractive but quite impossible in this climate before refrigeration. ● Dogs are kept as pets and working animals, but this poodle comes from late in the 20th century. ● A radio-controlled car cannot be a toy thousands of years before cars have been invented. ● The shopping cart will be more at home in the 20th century than in an Egyptian market. ● Wealthy Egyptian women use make-up and wear elaborate hairstyles, but without electricity, they cannot use a hairdrier. ● The Egyptians make beautiful glass items, but the tumbler and drinking straw are from the 20th century.
- Egyptian carts have wooden wheels. The pneumatic tire will not be invented until 1845.
- The time portal is in the pool in the center of the garden.

TIME ZONE 2: ROME, ITALY AD 100

- Your cyberform is standing in the center of the picture at the back, wearing a toga, and holding a shiny jar.
- Printing will not be used in Europe until the 15th century. Newspapers cannot yet be produced. ● The Romans use early dumbbells for developing their muscles, but these are 20th-century versions. ● The sports bag is from the 1980s. Apart from anything else, the zipper will not be invented until 1891. ● The Romans enjoy many kinds of ball games, but the racket dates from the 20th century. ● The Romans wear sandals or boots. The lace-up shoes belong to the 1950s. ● The Romans wear very little when exercising—this is a late 20th-century tracksuit. ● The plastic duck cannot exist before the development of plastics in the 20th century. ● Although the Chinese are probably drinking tea at this date, tea pots will not reach Europe for hundreds of years. ● The top hat belongs to a 19th-century gentleman, not a Roman senator. ● The mirror also belongs to the 20th century. The Romans make beautiful glass objects but cannot produce large sheets of glass.
- The Romans would not have kept their belongings in 20th-century lockers. ● The Romans have very efficient plumbing, but this toilet comes from the 1960s. ● The electric shower cannot be of much use 1800 years before the development of electrical appliances.
- "Exit" is a Latin word but this electric sign is from the 20th century. ● A revolving door will be more at home in the late 19th century. ● The Romans enjoy music, but they cannot have a jukebox in their baths. ● The Romans cannot wear plastic shower caps. ● The exercise bicycle definitely dates from the late 20th century. ● An inflatable mattress cannot exist 1600 years before plastics are in common use. ● Exactly the same can be said of the inflatable beach ball.
- The time portal is in the water, right at the front of the picture.

Time Zone 3: Lindisfarne, Britain 793

Time Zone 4: Chartres, France 1218

● Your cyberform is a monk, running with a silver plate, at the far right of the picture.
● Viking ships are open to the weather. They have no need of portholes. ● A light inflatable boat would be useful for landing, but rubber will not be used in Europe until the 17th century. ● The Vikings cannot use a modern fishing rod. Nylon fishing line will not be invented until the 1930s. ● Although the Vikings are fearsome fighters, pistols will not be made until the 16th century. ● In the days before firearms, there is no call for bullets! ● A windmill would certainly be useful—if the monks knew about electricity! ● It will not be until 1879 that Thomas Edison invents the electric light, so the Vikings cannot have mast lights.
● A floating buoy with an electric light on it is not available either. ● Nor is an electric flashlight. The first battery will be made in 1800 by Alessandro Volta. ● The Vikings use simple axes, not chainsaws, to fell the trees from which their boats are made. ● This is a modern Norwegian flag. The three nations of Norway, Sweden, and Denmark will not begin to emerge until the 900s. ● The monks might enjoy watching television but they will have to wait over 1100 years before it is invented! ● The first telescope will not be made until the early 1600s. ● Not even simple safety belts are available to make Viking voyages less dangerous. ● A tractor would make life easier for the monks, but the internal combustion engine will not be invented until the second half of the 19th century. ● Vikings aren't worried by the rain; steel frames for umbrellas will not be made until the late 19th century. ● No doubt the Vikings would be skillful windsurfers—but this is a hobby of the 20th century.
● The first food to be preserved in tin cans will not appear until 1810. ● Viking clothes are rough and hardwearing. The modern suit would not last long here! ● Putting rings on birds to track where they fly will not be done until the late 19th century.
● The time portal is within a cauldron in the center of a boat.

● Your cyberform is carrying a piece of glass, high up on one of the cathedral's towers.
● Over 600 years before the invention of the electric light, the new cathedral cannot be lit by spotlights. ● The pilgrims who flock to Chartres in the Middle Ages travel on foot or horseback, not in modern buses. ● Large sheets of plate glass will not be possible until the 17th century. ● Roads of this time are often rutted and muddy. Large highways only appear in the 20th century. ● Medieval sculptors carve stone statues and elaborate decorations, not abstract sculptures. ● Thefts from building sites cannot be prevented with wire-netting and barbed wire until the late 19th century. ● Electric amusement park rides cannot be enjoyed until well after the electric motor is developed in 600 years' time. ● Medieval children would love balloons, but the first one will not be made until 1783. ● The builders of the Middle Ages have to manage without powerful motorized machinery like this compressor. ● The steamroller will be invented in France—but not until 1859. ● Medieval builders use mortar, not cement, so do not use cement mixers! ● Large factories do not dominate the landscape until the late 18th century. ● The first iron suspension bridge will be built in 1880. Medieval bridges are built of stone or wood. ● Plastic piping will not be used until the 20th century.
● Ropes and pulleys are used to lift men and materials in the Middle Ages, but scaffolds like this are made from wood, not light aluminum or steel. ● There are stores in the 13th century, but not supermarkets like this one. ● Medieval workers enjoy social eating and drinking, but they do not sit down in modern cafés. ● Building sites always produce a lot of trash, but without a hydraulic crane to lift it, a dumpster would be of little use.
● Oxyacetylene tanks for electric welding are unknown in 1218. ● Advertising posters are not yet used as most people cannot read and printing has not yet been invented.
● The time portal is through one of the cathedral windows.

Time Zone 5: Florence, Italy 1492

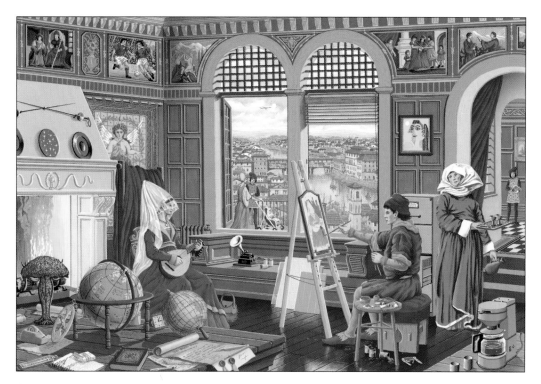

● Your cyberform is a servant standing at the far right of the picture.
● The elegant lamp dates from the end of the 19th century; in any case, it could not work without electricity. ● The tray is molded plastic, which will not be developed in a usable form until 1909. ● A spiral-bound notebook will not be produced until the 20th century.
● The traveling alarm clock belongs in the 20th century. ● The thermometer will be invented by an Italian, Galileo, but not for another hundred years. ● The dispenser for adhesive tape belongs on a desk of the 1990s, not the 1490s. ● Quill pens are in use at this date, not fountain pens. They will not be in common use until 1884. ● Tobacco will be one of the discoveries brought back to Europe from the Americas, but these cigarettes date from the 20th century. ● The first Venetian blind will not be produced until 1769. ● These Florentines do not have the luxury of central heating. The radiator belongs in the 20th century. ● This family's wealth is built on business, but metal filing cabinets will not be in common use for 450 years. ● Music is very popular, but the phonograph will not be introduced by Thomas Edison until 1877. ● Italian leatherwork is renowned in our own time, but this handbag dates from the 1960s. ● Italian knives and swords are famous too, but the penknife dates from the 20th century. ● Artists have to grind and mix their own paints. They cannot be bought in tubes until the 19th century. ● Coffee will be a well-loved drink in Europe in the future, but at this date it is drunk mainly in Africa. ● The baby and stroller are definitely from the late 20th century. ● Great patrons of the arts in 15th-century Florence probably won't appreciate the work of Picasso from the 20th century. ● Early ball games are being played at this date, but the wall painting shows soccer teams from the 1990s. ● Passengers will not be able to travel in the airplane flying above Florence until the first half of the 20th century.
● The time portal is through one of the shiny plates above the fireplace.

Time Zone 6: Tenochtitlan, Mexico 1519

● Your cyberform wears a medallion, and sits on his father's shoulders behind a Spanish flag.
● Although the legend of the eagle and snake that appears on it is an Aztec one, the flag on the right is that of modern Mexico. ● The fire hydrant dates from the 1900s. ● Cortés is certainly thinking of his business interests, but the attaché case is a 20th-century one. ● No Spanish soldier has yet seen a map of all the Americas, as most of the continent has not yet been discovered by Europeans. ● The oil lamp dates from the 19th century. ● Although the Aztecs play fast and furious ball games, they do not have 20th-century sneakers like these.
● Nor do the Aztecs' ball games use a modern basketball hoop. ● Although the game of golf is already being played in an early form, these clubs are certainly modern ones.
● A protective helmet might prove useful in the fighting to come, but this motorbike helmet comes from the 20th century. ● The Aztecs travel along their canals by canoe. The Spanish have arrived in wooden ships. But this ocean liner dates from the 20th century. ● Of course the Aztecs cook and heat their homes with fires, but this is a modern brick chimney pot.
● The sash window comes from an 18th-century house. ● Traffic lights might be useful for the busy canals of Tenochtitlán, but they cannot work without electricity. ● Not until the 19th century will babies be able to be pushed along in a baby carriage. ● The telegraph will not come into use until the first half of the 19th century, so there is no need for telegraph poles and wires now. ● The binoculars date from the 20th century. Even these cannot help the Aztecs to see into the future. ● Useful as it might be, the lifejacket will not be available for over 300 years. ● The Aztec child is playing with a 20th-century toy yacht. ● Barbed wire will not be invented in the USA until 1873. ● In this era grass is kept short by grazing animals. Mechanical lawnmowers will not come into use until the 19th century.
● The time portal is through the feathered shield on Montezuma's litter.

● Your cyberform is bowing to a samurai, in the center of the picture, holding a metal tray.
● The Japanese are used to cooking over hot embers, but this barbecue dates from the 20th century. ● Colored lanterns, not colored lights, line the streets during Japanese festivals before electricity is widely available. ● The baggage cart awaits the age of the airplane.
● Beautifully painted paper fans keep the Japanese cool. The electric fan is hundreds of years before its time. ● Air travel is still only for the birds. It will not be until 1783 that the French Montgolfier brothers make the first balloon flight. ● The Japanese cannot have a 20th-century clipboard. ● The saxophone will not be invented until the 1840s by Adolphe Sax, a Belgian. ● Canned food is not yet available. The method will first be used in 1810. ● Not until 1945 will American engineer Percy Le Baron Spencer discover that microwaves can be used for heating food. ● The Japanese are great seamen, but this numbered sail belongs on a modern racing yacht. ● This modern tugboat for bringing larger ships in and out of the harbor has not yet replaced the muscle power of oarsmen! ● Without electricity, there is little use for a 20th-century electric lamp. ● The Japanese and the Dutch have clerks to keep their accounts and records, but the blue chair belongs in the 20th century. ● The Dutch are adventurous travelers, but this is a 20th-century suitcase. ● The luggage cart belongs at least 300 years in the future. ● A seltzer bottle would be more at home with cocktails in the 1940s. ● The Dutch traders may well have brought European clocks with them, but this one is definitely modern. ● Shoes with raised soles to keep feet clean on muddy roads are common, but it will not be until the 1960s that stiletto heels are fashionable. ● Lights to warn ships of danger are not unknown, but this lighthouse dates from the early 20th century.
● A radio tower is unnecessary hundreds of years before radio waves have been discovered.
● The time portal is a shiny metal plate at the foot of the ornate European chair.

● Your cyberform is the horseman with raised sword at the left of the picture.
● During the Revolution a 20th-century burglar alarm will offer no protection. ● John Logie Baird will first demonstrate television in 1926. TV cameras will appear later still.
● Electric loudspeaker systems are not yet available. The King's voice is drowned by the soldiers' drums. ● The thermos bottle dates from the 20th century. ● The revolutionaries have simple guns, but the machine gun is a 20th-century model. ● Newspapers are now growing in popularity, but the colorful magazine comes from the 1990s. ● The revolutionaries are campaigning, but not against nuclear weapons—the Campaign for Nuclear Disarmament badge is before its time. ● More than 50 years before the invention of the internal combustion engine, gas cans have no use. ● There are many imposing buildings in Paris, but high-rise apartments will not appear until the 20th century. ● A crane like this one will be a common sight in the second half of the 20th century but is out of place now. ● The mini skirt will not be seen on Paris streets until the 1960s. ● Parking meters will be invented in 1935 by the American C. C. Magee. ● It is a long time before the invention of tape-recording machines; the radio-interviewer has slipped back 150 years.
● Steelband drums will be made of oil drums when the internal combustion engine has made oil an important commodity. ● The plastic traffic cones are strictly a 20th-century sight.
● Baseball will first be played in the United States in 1839, but this baseball cap is of an even later date. ● The retractable dog leash is a 20th-century invention. ● Fast food in cartons will be common in the 20th century. ● Before the invention of the telephone or intercom, the door buzzer is certainly out of place. ● So many years before the invention of the internal combustion engine, car drivers will not need traffic signs.
● The time portal is through the carriage window.

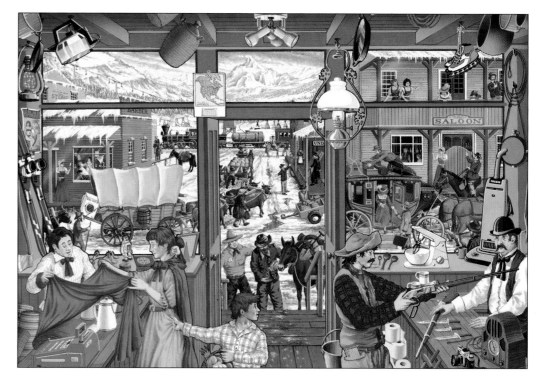

● Your cyberform is sharpening his scythe outside his cottage.
● There is no need for a gas pump as motor transport is still not available. ● In an age before cars, a parking lot is not really necessary! ● It will be more than 30 years before Thomas Edison invents the electric light. The streetlight is before its time. ● So is the carriage's flashing electric light. ● The elevator will not be invented until 1854. Neither the glass-sided elevator on the side of the building, nor the machine lifting workmen up the unfinished building are possible yet. ● The first pedal-operated bicycle will be made in the late 1830s but this is a much later model. ● In 1845 steam trains are running between Manchester and Liverpool, but the locomotive on the left dates from the late 20th century.
● A backhoe like this cannot be built until the first internal combustion engine is developed in 15 years' time. ● The modern combine harvester belongs to the 1970s. ● Round straw bales will not be seen in fields until farming is mechanized by the huge machines of the late 20th century. ● Portable office buildings are a feature of 20th-century building sites. ● Grain from these fields is stored in barns. Silos will be commonly used only in the 20th century.
● The child's model airplane is over a hundred years too early. ● As towns grow up, more and more people enjoy visits to the countryside. The hiker, however, belongs in the next century. ● Fire brigades do exist now but modern fire extinguishers are not yet in use.
● For travelers in trouble on the road, help is farther than a telephone call away. The earliest telephone will be made in 1876. ● The power lines are before their time. These mills are powered by steam. ● John Logie Baird will first demonstrate television in 1926. The cottage has no need of an antenna. ● Modern trailers are not available for holidays at this time, especially as there as yet are no cars to pull them!
● The time portal is in a drinking trough on the roadside.

● Your cyberform is the woman standing on the sidewalk holding a mirror.
● The days of the Pony Express are past and trains now take the mail, but airmail letters are not yet possible (there are no airplanes!). ● Although wind-up toys are very popular, this robot comes from the late 20th century. ● Cameras at this time are large and cumbersome, not portable like this modern one. ● Keeping a home clean is not easy before William Hoover begins manufacturing vacuum cleaners in the early 1900s. ● Cooking is hard work too—this foodmixer from the 1970s is no use without electricity! ● Sanitary arrangements here are fairly primitive, but even wealthy homes back East do not have soft rolls of toilet paper yet! ● Skiing dates back hundreds of years, but modern skis made of man-made materials will only be available in the second half of the 20th century. ● Oregon in 1876 is much bigger than it will be later. Several states have yet to acquire their 20th-century map boundaries. ● James Ritty of the U.S.A. will invent the cash register in 1879—electric ones will come later still. ● 1879 will also see the invention of the electric light. These spotlights are out of place. ● The roller blades are ahead of their time too. ● Wealthy people do take holidays, but jetting away to the sun is not yet possible! ● Without electricity in the home, this modern kettle is of little use. ● The discoveries that will make radio possible will begin in the 1890s, but this is definitely a 1950s radio. ● Petroleum has been discovered by now, but moving it is a problem as tanker trucks have not yet been developed. ● The trailer is for towing by car—several years before the earliest cars will be built. ● The first electric streetcar will be demonstrated in 1879. Electric chair lifts will follow even later. ● It is goldmines, not oil wells, that have attracted many early settlers. ● This hairdrier comes from the 1970s not the 1870s. ● The electric washing machine will not be invented until the early 1900s.
● The time portal is through a lamp hanging at the top left of the picture.

● Your cyberform is conducting a band on the dockside.
● Like the *Mauretania*, the *Queen Elizabeth II* will be a luxury liner, but her maiden voyage will not be until 1969. ● The first commercial airline is beginning this year in the US, but planes do not yet need proper airports with runways. ● Hang-gliding will not become a popular sport until the 1970s and '80s. ● Suffragettes campaign on the dockside for women to have the same rights as men. It is not yet possible for a woman to captain a liner. ● Women's clothes are very restrained—a modern swimsuit would be thought quite indecent.
● Dress codes for men are also conservative—Hawaiian shirts and shorts will not become popular until the 1950s. ● Although the first tank will be built in 1916, the poster shows a much later version. ● The walkie talkie two-way radio will not be seen for several decades.
● Although the *Mauretania* is fitted with one of the latest radio telephones, the one here is clearly a much later model. ● The speedboat belongs to the 1970s, not 1914. ● The security camera is electronically controlled. It will not be available until the late 20th century.
● Although a simple idea, skateboards will not become popular with children until the 1970s. ● The first oil well was drilled on land in the 1850s, but it will not be until the middle of the 20th century that drilling begins at sea. ● Europe is about to be plunged into war. The European Union flag, symbolizing unity, is far in the future. ● It will not be until the 1980s that vacationers can use video cameras. ● Motor vehicles are in use, but this tractor trailer will not appear on the dockside until the 1970s. ● Forklift trucks will not become a common feature in loading bays until the 1960s. ● Plastic credit cards will not be in use until the 1970s. ● The passenger wearing a Walkman will need to wait until 1979 before he can buy one. ● It will be about twenty years before radar is developed.
● The time portal is in the water between the dock and the ship's side.

● Your cyberform is passing a can of film up to an assistant.
● Electronically operated digital clocks and watches will not be widely available until the 1970s. ● The first serviceable helicopter will not be flown until the late 1930s. ● Satellite dishes to receive television programs will not be in common use until the 1980s. ● The space shuttle will first be built in 1976; after years of development it will finally be launched in 1981. ● Although motorcycles are a popular means of transport, this one belongs in the 1970s. ● Scuba gear will not be invented until the 1940s. ● Cars are an important status symbol for the rich and famous but this sports car won't be around until the 1970s.
● The first commercial flight of the supersonic Concorde airplane will not be until 1976.
● Cans of spray paint will not replace the paintbrush until the 1940s. ● This radio cassette player will not be in the shops until the 1980s. ● It is still considered rather glamorous to be seen smoking. The terrible damage that it does to health will not be widely recognized for several years. ● J. F. Kennedy, 35th President of the United States, is only 19 years old in 1936, and his brother Robert is 11. ● The use of electronic keyboards to create sounds will be a feature of music in the 1980s. ● The microchip has not yet made portable personal communicators possible. The first portable telephones will not be available until as late as 1986. ● The first microprocessor-based computer will be developed in 1974. In 1936 there is still a great deal of paperwork! ● The electronics needed to build a sophisticated vending machine are still in the future. ● Ian Fleming's first James Bond novel will be published in 1953. The famous 007 will star in films of the future. ● In 1936 Elvis Presley is only one year old! ● The polaroid camera, able to develop its own prints, will not be developed until the 1940s. ● Pocket calculators using microchip technology will not appear until the early 1970s.
● The time portal is through a light, hanging from the ceiling.

● The baby stroller returned from Florence in 1492, but without the child. ● The clothes should be in the suitcase located in Nagasaki in 1633. ● The radio interviewer has retrieved everything from Paris, in 1793, except his microphone. ● The woman at the table should be reading either the woman's magazine from Paris, in 1793, or the newspaper from Rome, in AD 100. ● The caller needs a telephone handset like the one from the ship-to-shore radio on the *Mauretania* in Liverpool, in 1914. ● The guitarist lacks his guitar. It has failed to return from Thebes, in 1400 BC. ● Somewhere in space a poodle is lost! The last time you saw it was also in Thebes. ● A tray has disappeared from the traveler's hand. It was in Florence, in 1492. ● A woman has lost her luggage cart. You saw it in Nagasaki, in 1633. ● The vehicle is missing its wheels! The pneumatic tires were last seen in Thebes, in 1400 BC. ● The scaffolding cradle needed for the cleaner to stand on has not arrived from Chartres, in 1218. ● A woman still needs her notebook. You saw it in Florence, in 1492. ● A chair is missing from the table. It was lost on the return journey from Nagasaki, in 1633. ● The glass from which the passenger is drinking has not returned from Thebes, in 1400 BC. ● The smoke comes from missing factory chimneys. You saw them outside Chartres, in 1218. ● The helicopter is in grave danger without its rotor blades. They have not returned from Hollywood, in 1936. ● The traveler is missing his backpack. You may remember it from Manchester, in 1845. ● The luggage is missing its baggage cart. You saw it in Nagasaki, in 1633. ● There is no chance of the airplane taking off with only one wing. Most of the plane returned from Florence, in 1492. ● Defying gravity, the flag flies without a flagpole. You should remember it from the dockside in Liverpool, in 1914. ● The time portal is through the roof of the travel shop.

A Puzzle from Times Past

● The object you have not already encountered is concerned with time: it is the hourglass.